LAMPBLAC

LAMPBLACK&ASH

Simone Muench

**Winner of the 2004
Kathryn A. Morton Prize in Poetry
Selected by Carol Muske-Dukes**

SARABANDE BOOKS
LOUISVILLE, KENTUCKY

Managing Editor
Sarabande Books, Inc.
2234 Dundee Road, Suite 200
Louisville, KY 40205

Library of Congress Cataloging-in-Publication Data

Muench, Simone, 1969–
    Lampblack and ash : poems / by Simone Muench ; selected by Carol
Muske-Dukes.—1st ed.
        p.   cm.
    "Winner of the 2004 Kathryn A. Morton Prize in Poetry."
    ISBN 1-932511-26-1 (cloth : alk. paper) — ISBN 1-932511-27-X (pbk. :
alk. paper)
    I. Muske-Dukes, Carol, 1945– II. Title.
PS3563.U358L36 2005
811'.6—dc22   2005002565

13-digit ISBN: 978-1-932-51126-0 (cloth); 978-1-932-51127-7 (paper)

Cover image: Wesley Kimler, *Giant Insect Detail*, black gesso/charcoal on paper

Cover and text design by Charles Casey Martin

Manufactured in the United States of America.
This book is printed on acid-free paper.

Sarabande Books is a nonprofit literary organization.

Partial funding has been provided by the Kentucky Arts Council, a state
agency in the Commerce Cabinet, with support from the National
Endowment for the Arts.

For
Lanko, Stephanie and Bill, for your grip and your grace
and for
Retta, Jesse, John, and Kevin

CONTENTS

III. THE SKY'S SONG

ACKNOWLEDGMENTS

Much gratitude to the editors and staff of the following journals for first publishing these poems:

Bellingham Review: "The Laws of Sawdust and Stars," "Robert Desnos and the Hummingbird," and "Window"

Blue Sky Review: "Residue"

The Common Review: "The Siren's Dream"

Diagram: "Elegy for the Unsaid" and "Freeze Frame, with Forsythia"

Fourteen Hills: "Hydrophobia"

GSU Review: "Ore"

Indiana Review: "Pretty White Dress"

Konundrum Engine Literary Review: "One Swallow Doesn't Make a Summer"

Mot Juste: "Viewing Rain from a Hospital Bed"

Notre Dame Review: "The *Melos* of Medusa"

The Paris Review: "*In Medias Res*"

Poetry Center of Chicago: "There Are Wolves that Sit at the Feet of Men"

Poetry Society of America (Poetry in Motion): "Why Women Don't Wear Silk Aprons"

Pleiades: "Sketches of Dresses in Mean Reds"

Poetry: "The OED Defines Red-Hot"

Pool: "I'm Like You, My Dear" (published as "Shadowgraphs")

Rattle: "What We Were Told"

Rhino: "The Sky's Song" (translation)

River City: "By Your Mouth"

Runes: "Terroir"

Samizdat: "The Disease of Pronouns" and "In the Coppice"

Scene 360: "Courting Procrustes"

Swink: "Spectacle: Possession"

Third Coast: "The Insinuation of Lakes in the 'The Garden of
  Mourners'"

"Robert Desnos and the Hummingbird" received the AWP Intro
Journal Award. "Window" won the 49th Parallel Award judged
by Robert Wrigley. "Why Women Don't Wear Silk Aprons" won
the Fine Lines Contest sponsored by Olay and the PSA, judged
by Sonia Sonchez, Sandra Cisneros, Sapphire, Lee Ann Brown,
Jill Bialosky, Julia Alvarez, and Marilyn Chin. "By Your Mouth"
was selected by Anne Waldman for 1st place in the 9th Annual
Juried Reading in Chicago. "Elegy for the Unsaid" appeared as
a broadside for The Chicago Poetry Center's New American
Poets Series, and is anthologized in *Red, White, and Blues: Poets
on the Promise of America* edited by Ryan G. Van Cleave and
Virgil Suarez. Chicagopoetry.com anthologized *"In Medias Res."*
The first section of "Spectacle: Possession" appears on the CD
reVerse produced by Kenneth Clarke and Richard Fammeree.

Abundant thanks to all those listed above, as well as *Poetry
Daily, Verse Daily, Melic Review, Lily, Wicked Alice, Windows,*
Paul Breslin, The Poetry Center, *ChicagoPoetry* and *Words on
Walls* for circulating many of my poems. Thanks to Ander
Monson at *Diagram* for first publishing some of these poems in
the chapbook *Notebook. Knife. Mentholatum.* Thanks to the
Illinois Arts Council who provided support for the completion of
this manuscript.

Love and gratitude to Lanko Miyazaki, Stephanie McCanles,
Bill Mondi, Wesley Kimler, and Seth Cohen for holding my hand
through the mustard; to Kevin Smith, Kristy Odelius, Mary
Biddinger, Jackie White, Ariana-Sophia Kartsonis, Michael
Anania, and Anne Winters for their expert editorial advice; and to
the *ACM* staff and Chicago Women's Poetry Group for their title
assistance. Finally, thanks to Carol Muske-Dukes for selecting.

INTRODUCTION

Alll poetry lies somewhere between augury and obsession. Though she asks, "Who believes in auguries anymore?" Simone Muench in *Lampblack & Ash* answers her own question unhesitatingly in these hermetic yet direct poems which speak to the reader like high-speed oracles.

Still, there is something utterly in thrall here, honey-slow and fixated. Driven by obsession—in particular, obsession with the legendary French poet, Robert Desnos—Muench's identification with a true self beyond the self's known truth is startling. Contemporary poetic consciousness, bristling as it is with a sense of the territorial, the owned, is not accustomed to this intensity of hero-worship, this informed adulation. "He was more delicate than eyelids / but nobler than a soldier."

Yet we quickly grow accustomed to the working necessity of her homage. For the lineaments of Desnos' desires and her own deeply mirror each other, twinning up into an exhilarating style that outdistances both the conventions of "persona" and the melodrama of "possession." Through this alignment, Muench is allowed freedom to construct the new in much the same manner that Desnos' famous experiments in automatic writing animated his own brilliantly speculative efforts.

This is not a matter of worshipful mimesis: "I want you to see *me,* to stop / pursuing my image" she shouts as an ironical Medusa —pointing to what permits the poem to do its work, the act of recovery of the once and still real. These are *her* poems, her illuminations. Just as the invisible hand that moves the pen will not ultimately suffice, just as Desnos found it necessary to break free of surrealistic montage and into "real" speech, Muench's refusal to pursue the image for its own sake moves her into something further: "...a mirror fragment" but one "containing the tumult of water / and bodies."

What Muench does in these poems is what, in fact, all poets purport to do—that is to say, talk to the dead, let the dead speak—then offer answers. Muench has taken on Desnos' mannerisms, his colors, his recklessly gorgeous polyphonic music and made them uniquely her own—something beyond "answering":

> past the shoulder where the cicatrix of a small
> pox shot identifies. Blue skin. Blue sky.

An ice skate will float by on her "river," but it floats by on "the river's ear," a synthesis so inspired it feels new-made. The poems are vertiginously inventive even as they are immensely sayable, thinkable, and very funny:

> you're less lovely in the light
> but lovelier than last night when you
> heaved over the side of a yacht
>
> into your own moon-mad reflection

Muench is adept at "transmitting the arbitrary fragments of the unconscious," but more adept at integrating them. The depth of identification with mastery, with enormous grief and enormous optimism and joy, becomes her force field.

> You are a reticulation
>   in my skin, Euclidian.
>   A warning, apiarian, you
>
> are the keeper of bees.

The dualities are meant to call attention to themselves as they are erased—augury to obsession to image. In poem after poem, Muench calls up the sheer resistance of the soul to all attempts to bind it to time. The awful beauty of a rapist's skin, gamblers trading organs for gold, a trampoline, a silver screw undoing what we thought we knew of tomorrow—these are her unbindings.

One recalls the image of Desnos reading the palms of other inmates at Buchenwald near the end of his life. Before the forced march to Terezin, before the typhus that claimed him at the moment of liberation—he promised each one of them happiness, prosperity, long life. As with all fruitions of the psyche, as with the remarkable, glorious poems of Simone Muench—the future was meant to be. In what time, in what limiting when, is not the concern of either poet or poem. What concerns the poet here is how we see through all things, even the future—to a "Blue door on a black house, your body/like glass: a pitcher of violets, twilight, a blue fruit/abandoned."

—Carol Muske-Dukes

I.

UNDRESS

undress yourself
bathe in this black water
you have nothing to fear
you've already done it
the human body is waterproof
—Robert Desnos

I'm Like You, My Dear

I'm like you, my dear,
a leafleteer of belle-lettres.
A fan of lentissimo,

doloroso.

Leeks and lemon verbena.

A funambulist with zero
visibility.

I'm blue sugar
on the lunar line. Iron
pyrite and diamondbacks.

Luminescent,

nascent. A shell pink
shack. I'm the lot
you draw, the hammock

where you sip elixirs
in exile. Where whitetails
forage the yard, tearing up
dogtooth violets.

A geography
of gypsum and hooves.

I'm like you, my dear.
Though you're a fig tree borer
and I'm a goldfinch watching you
funnel your way through my home.

Like virga you disappear
before I even reach your shadow.
Though you leave a residue,

texture of red

falling across the unsung
country of Arkansas. Light
like a woman's sleeve
sweeping over the field.

I'm like you, my dear. Just a little
too near the Scylla. Sea-
level and singing
a cappella.

Robert Desnos and the Hummingbird

A poem about you would begin with a tiger, a cobra,
a salami sandwich, it would contain
taxonomic terms for woody plants: *sessile, catkin,*
schizocarp, dehiscent, involucre, whorl;
it would cruise rue Saint-Martin and pick up chicks
at the *Musée de l'Orangerie* between marble busts
of Etruscan warriors, a poem about you
would go everywhere, and never arrive.
It would list a series of phobias:
ailurophobia fear of cats
erythrophobia fear of red
nostophobia fear of returning home
It would indulge in hyperbole: you are as exotic
as an ocelot, or the merge of an abacus
with a hummingbird—a moving scale of song.
A poem about you would include an obituary,
Compiègne, Havana, rumba, tango,
plums, the language of pain which has no letters,
only cells and vortexes; however, a poem about pain
would not be a poem about you.
It would speak of the heart though,
not as symbol but as organ and orator
of the body's blood. Its hollow muscularity
and conical shape, obliquely placed,
its *vena cava and auriculo-ventricular groove;*
endocardium, myocardium, pericardium.
A poem about you would switch subjects
suddenly and lilt word duets: creeper vine,

adder's tongue. It would contemplate
the prepositional phrase and carry the glare of stars
beneath the innuendoes of trees. It would abound
with women: Madeleine, Yvonne, Youki.
A poem about you would tell a story about a girl
who one night while steeping tea, spilled
honey on a book and discovered you.
In the end every poem is drenched
with honey and history and so the girl
leaned near the window with violet light
falling through like liquid and wrote a poem
to you called
                    Crepuscule

        A hummingbird quivers near my ear:
        wind singed with sumac, the dusky
        sibilance of your name: *Desnos,*
        Desnos. Sky thick with cumulonimbus and
        the whining of blue jays. How odd
        to never hold the heft of you
        knowing already your absence, like echo
        and snow, but to think of this
        is to sink into a subterranean landscape
        of crows and curses. Permit me
        the traffic of a broken heart.
        Blue slate of this day stains
        my dress, but the rain's veneer is beautiful
        and contains the language of lost causes.
        Such lassitude in this wet darkness—lamps
        locate bodies like pearls
        rolling across a dresser. Light
        diffracts through my glasses in the rain—

a microscopic slide of amoeba
that glitters in my periphery. Every word spoken
is a city sunk beneath a verdigris sea.
My heart is full of seaplants smelling
like lead and laundry.
Wet bark skimming my spine while
rivulets write your words upon my bodice:
J'ai tant rêvé de toi que tu perds ta réalité.

There Are Wolves that Sit at the Feet of Men

there are lakes that spin rain into constellations
highways that switch into rivers
gamblers who trade organs for gold

there are fiddles that can kill you
carving their song *la cienaga* into arms
until it's a flesh-yelling circle

of loup-garous and you
perched like a comma in the middle
of a sentence, circumscribed but alive

the word is a broken door
where light slips through like indium,
scattering the thousand prisms of self

there are cicadas that decay into lace,
indian burns from girls in third grade
whose crushes translate to sugar and ice

imbalance of sentimentality

you're less lovely in the light
but lovelier than last night when you
heaved over the side of a yacht

into your own moon-mad reflection
as frost formed on the sea,
and fish slipped through

ice cracks: mercury-lit filaments

listen to the fricative sigh
of fingers through tresses,
over peaches that glow

like low-watt bulbs
and locate the different hues
of blue in your boneblack hair

there are wrinkles like
scrawls of a suicide note,
infinite rose slopes

of snow, a gaze through violet
haze of leaf smoke as the swallow
leaves its shadow

in melted tallow—a grey smear,
imprint of bird feet, impossible feat
of flying through resin

wings fling open evening, amber-
stained, stars hung over the sea like letters
of your name which is invisible

except on the liminal highways
of a woman's thighs and
the snake eyes of battered dice

The Laws of Sawdust and Stars

Who knows how it's done.
You don't have to believe in ghosts
or God. Something moves

in the forest beyond the garden. A man
opens his door to a witch
disguised as a stem of snapdragons

that flush his skin with fever.
She comes again, dressed as a tropical wind.
Water on skin, he glistens

with indecision. He wants to climb
through the window into the woods
to spin the witch into a woman

but he's in charge of repairing a roomful
of clocks that no longer tick-tock
but reel a tune like a jewelry box.

Cumulus, ruffled as jabots, muffle the moon's
sallow light. The laws of sawdust and stars say:
close your eyes till you hear rain, follow

its moss and metal smell, as it turns
evening's debris into silverroot, and peaches
light the path to a city built on a sea of mercury.

A telegram sends news of his disappearance.
It was really the somber notes of crows,
but who believes in auguries anymore?

We wait at our own windows for his story.
Perhaps scrawled in the margins of the book
he was reading, dog-eared and coffee-spilled;

or scratched with a safety pin
on the headboard; or maybe
his story is recorded in the songs

of broken clocks that divulge:
he was more delicate than eyelids,
but nobler than a soldier.

Drowning by the Light of Oranges

I pinned a star
      on the shadow
            of your shoulder.

It sucked darkness
      into a mandarin flame
            where you leaned

against a boat
      overflowing with ice
            and oranges. You're

a pinned flame,
      an asterisk of snow
            disappearing in the thin

isolation of my dress;
      in nightcrush and suck,
            ice shines

metal flowers.
      The river carries stars.
            Fish bones flicker

beneath the surface
      littered with trout silk
            and snow.

Your shoulder aligns
        itself with the stars—
                orange light isolates

shadows of boats
        that appear flickering
                silk on the ice-

flowered river. I go under
        the snow's crush, an
                asterisk pinned in by

your shoulder. Your shadow.

Sketches of Dresses in Mean Reds

1

In an orange dress proclaiming flame
Pain says, *Baby, this is how it's gonna be.*

She begins almost innocuously: a paper cut,
a corn; then gallstones, daughter's dog

beneath the wheel of the Mercury Marquis.
Suddenly, your house is burning down.

It's the build-up, breakdown of body that excites
as she pricks loved ones with her lethal

needle. If you're still, quiet as spite
Pain purses her lips and blows you a goodbye kiss;

places a pistol in your hand and singsongs
in your ear: *Here. Hold this. Feel this.*

2

No two shoulders are alike; no two trees
have the same leaves though it's deceiving:

infinite pattern of palms, fingertips that lift
a spaghetti strap from the clavicle, lower

past the shoulder where the cicatrix of a small
pox shot identifies. Blue skin. Blue sky.

Pick-up truck. Texas on a Sunday afternoon.
To think one shouldn't don black in summer.

The dead still smell and collect the river's
detritus in tangled tresses, surprised mouths.

In front of a church, an uprising of skirts
as choir girls congregate for a photograph.

White sashes cinch thin waists. Lily-of-the-valley
in their hair. Farther down the river, willow leaves

stick to the foreheads of two girls. Dresses—wet
feathers pressed to flawless backs.

3
Through indigo windows,
women bent over ironing

boards, reserved
as pearls, pressing

dresses for a funeral.
Still life of lemons

moonlit in the cool
dark kitchen. Not yet

lit by sun or lamp. Iris hue.
Lover, there is no getting

over beyond this,
only plum and thistle.

The OED Defines Red-Hot

She's a hot tomato; love-
apple; Marilyn Monroe's
mink stole. *Different guys*
have different names for dolls,
such as broads, tomatoes.
She's the woman
loitering in the harbor. Rhapsodic.
She's bloodshot and bittersweet.
Cerise

streak across her cheeks. Blood-
blistered. Auburn hair. She lingers
in the arbor beneath mimosa trees,
sipping Madeira, stuffing
currants in her carmine
mouth. She's rosy. Rusty.
Ready.

She's a red-lighter; a scarlet
starlet. She wears school-girl
socks. A red fox.
A fox is a girl.
A fox is a chick, you see?
She's sweet as pink
zabaglione. Steak tartar
a la carte. She's brick
and blush; damask,
dangerous.

Both rose and solferina, she
drives a station wagon, plagued
by cherry air freshener and too-tight
puce shoes, her skin a detonating fuse.
She's blowzy, a cardinal flower.
Cinnabar scent. Terra-cotta.
Copper.

From chestnut to cherry, she's
your edible lady. A pepper,
a snapper, a strawberry.
Red puccoon.
There's some red-hot ones
up—you know where—in Piccadilly.
Pink as lox, flush
of lobster. She's a risk
and a rush. Firewater.
Lava.

She bristles and bridles
in a vermeil seizure.
The bride-to-be is probably
some frightful red-hot
momma. She's *coral nails,*
crimson lips. Geranium
windowsill. She's a rubified rubric.
She's you and your. Abused
and suffused. Marooned in red.
Tinted woman. Caught in
a Pompeii cauldron of poppies,
rubies: a red-hot
sex-pot.

By Your Mouth

At night I sleep with the saddest men

but today I ache, moths and blood
decorating my bed, a conjuring

trick I shrink
my spine into. My wrists

raw wool and black
as malpractice from your bite.

Today, not even a meteor swarm
can alarm me.

My hands bare the bad lands,
molded riot of Texas

purple spike. Debut of the mad
muse—how like spies it is disguised.

Outdoors, the wars roar on and
the dead are gathered

like promissory notes and buried
in their grandmothers' mink coats.

——

You salute with a broken tooth, words
tapering off, vapor lifting out your eyes,
no longer knowing the difference between
photographs and mirrors. Shadows border
lips, the severe sheerness of your existence.
Call in the maintenance staff for your removal.
You're a groove in my lineage, a greasy spoon
where I consumed eggs overeasy. The sun's
just a rerun. I'd come to your funeral
if I were in a better mood, but my head jerks
with a thousand whipsnakes. When you died,
I swooned like a flamenco dancer on Acapulco
gold while honey guides and vinegar flies gathered
near your stain, small as bird shadow, on the snow.

———

Days when I gaze into your glass
eye, archeological remains

of your tortured back, mustangs
gather at your open mouth.

You conspire against my pleasure,
your sadness is ferocious, taller

than Kilimanjaro. You live in my ribs,
a ruby boutonnière; you are plum

and pendulum; a car salesman in white
tie and tails. You're bizarre as innards,

buzzards as you stumble dream
to dream you reside in margins,

in the blurry vision of virgins;
in my eyes, you are aniline dye,

the deep south of your contagious mouth.

Viewing Rain from a Hospital Bed

Something sidles
up to me in the dark, I

taste it; this disease
I can't speak.

I listen to rain, tangled
branches, scar on my chest.

It shoots. You
lick it.

How is it? Don't go
where you don't belong.

It's how you hear it—
scar, emblem of chance,

unnameable odor
pearling out of it

and over you,
stifling you in bed.

But what if
like an axolotl, its

quickness I visit,
and slip coiling into light?

Not scar, not
that voice

of ache and tomorrow; or bone
crack for having moved too fast.

What if held beneath sea
it turned a beautiful

blue, an impenetrable
blue? Could all that liquid

be the source of fall?
Here beneath flesh: is an I

with diamond bones, some
split in rot, others

rain sparks, sage
blooming additions. Here it ends—

could I erase
in lampblack rain,

the moon flickering?

In Medias Res

Some nights are as black
as belladonna—the black that gathers
at the back of the throat when a boy's
voice falls over your head like a hood:
Don't scream or I'll kill you.

Black of shadows, pupils
that dilate as you stare at each other, stock
still as this memory, almost as if
you were in love,
in front of a house where pizzicato

of drizzle on a tin roof is a metronome.
Intercostal placement
of the blade. More precisely,
I'll gut you like a fish if you make a move.
The blues are no refuge

filtering out of a nearby bar like a confession
when your life is before you or over
in one quick flick of a muscular wrist.
I've killed before, you know?
I won't refute it. Your loot

is my watch, twenty bucks, a rhinestone
choker, and my death
which has yet to be decided.

Through all of this I can't
help but think what perfect

skin you have. Later, the cops
will laugh at this
as we drive the grid of blocks
searching for you. Sourness
of the late hour smelling of henbane

that loiters in the mouth, on skin,
even in the leather of boots
and belts, the casings of blades.
You're pretty, lucky for you I let you live.

II.

UNDER THE WILLOWS

...When the time comes everything will happen transparently
more renowned than the aviary where the feathers are scattered
A celebrated tree rises above the world with
hanged men deep in its earthbound roots
It is this day that I choose....

—Robert Desnos

Elegy for the Unsaid

after Neruda

In this mouth I gather darkness, an aria,
rosewater tongue, tympanic bone,
a poem more quiet than quietness,
a bronze song, something undone, salvia,
a crushed butterfly.
It is the blood on a light bulb, the seventh sadness,
a fluctuation that closes oceans and eyes.
The vermilion and solitary luminary
shimmies and singes the feathers of the aviary.

Moon, the clock's word, dear country, ruin, rain.

Window

Call me a tiger the boy said. His mouth, wine-
lacquered, damp and deep pink; pomegranate

purse of his lips, a tart knot of inexperience.
I used my fingers to pry his mouth open, red velvet

interior of my mother's jewelry box;
something precious I wasn't allowed to touch

so I went looking for what was hidden
in men: shadows and odors, their

mouths. Curtained entry into a magenta
bordello: whip-brush of tongue, its salt

and saliva; teeth and their tendency
to draw blood. I loved most the jaw:

mandible and maxilla, the way
they opened the mouth like a window

I could crawl through after curfew
into night's bruises and pearl light, swallowing

Boone's Farm, and pulling my clothes off
in petals: *he loves me, he loves me not.*

When I slipped back into my room, I knew
my mother would be waiting, hairbrush in hand

to beat desire from me. After, I'd lie awake,
listen to mice, tiny bones as they crunched

in the mouth of my cat, my mother weeping
in her sleep as moonlight settled like ice

on the window with teeth, with eyes.

In the Coppice

I waited in the coppice
        for you. Country of wrong, country of
                despair & bad weather we remain

for the sundries the rain brings
        in bowls & glass-bottom boats—
                purple-whelk, thulite, peach

blossoms & hornblende.
        Your castellated figure
                wears yellow while violets

leak from your eyes. Your heels
        full of constellations send you
                reeling through the underwood.

Cumulus grate against the sky
        swifter than your fleet-
                footed grace as you follow

your own shadow lit by mirrors
        on the backs of birds. You are
                a phosphene—brilliant irritant

in my eye; like yellow-banded
        clouds thick as wax, you attract
                hummingbirds & honey buzzards.

You are a reticulation
    in my skin, Euclidian.
        A warning, apiarian, you

are the keeper of bees. I covered
    my flesh with pollen & straw,
        with kohl-rimmed lids I came to you

in the coppice where you hid
    your ductility, gold-green
        winged & veined. Leaf

spill, yellow odor
    on your collar. I pull you closer
        to smell the centuries. You are archaic

& I am archival.

What We Were Told

The beautiful woman in front of you
is not your wife
though you'd like her to be.
You woo her with bouquets
from the garden every day.

She insists on a list and to your astonishment
the names fly out of your mouth
with the speed of hummingbird wings:
agastache, scarlet gilia, cosmos.
You're an architect

of petals. You tell her you'll twist wisteria,
the scented limbs of cherry trees
into a home. You assemble a gazebo
of leaves for her to wait
while you erect your castle of flowers. Of course,

you will fail. You were never told every fairy tale
is tinged with soot. Look back
over your shoulder
already the woman is dismantling
your carefully constructed hut, the flowers

in your hand have wilted, the castle's caving in.
A few startled birds flutter in the air,

your voice calling after her.
That's all that's left
and nothing else.

Why Women Don't Wear Silk Aprons

Under villanelles of pleated dresses women forget flesh.
—Yusef Komunyakaa

In Louisiana swamplight where highway
hasn't hit Iota, boys dig for crawfish,
articulation buried in a weather chart,
while girls gather laundry from the levee,
knee-deep in devil's walking stick.
Here, even petite women master
how to swing a hoe and chop
a chicken's head off in one graceful blow.
Through the vignettes of velvet legs,
men remember mothers. Down
the road, combines thresh rice fields,
while women bend their spines,
shake turnips from furrowed dirt
and hang silk stockings on a line.

The Melos of Medusa

It's the jitters that give them a hard-on!
—Hélène Cixous

I once was a beautiful woman;
       now it's come down to tricks and stones,
           the wick of my voice sputtering

curses in the Mediterranean breeze.
       I once believed that voice
           was sustenance: beauty and weight

of a pomegranate—its wine-colored chambers,
       a thousand rooms to lose
           yourself in. Now I know

no one was listening but the goats
       as they ate their way through night's
           detritus: an orgy where men sang

and drank while women, thin as mist,
       whispered on the periphery. *Lovely*
           mouths gagged with pollen.

Perseus, as you move your back
       toward me, I want to lick
           the delicate skin where armor

doesn't sheath the elegance
       of your neck as you peruse
           my reflection in your shield.

I want you to see *me,* to stop
 pursuing my image. It wasn't my face
  that turned those poor men to rock.

It was the burn of me—even
 my navel, a thimble of fire. My hair,
  a catastrophe of fiery curls, not coils

of water moccasins. But the myth remains
 the same: someone is saved; someone
  dies a terrible death.

We know the rules.
 My song that has gone so long
  unheard will taunt you in your sleep

even as you sweep your sword
 across my neck like a finger
  tracing its own silence.

Ore

Sing me a least harmonic song, a song that is fierce
to the ear: and read to me in French, Creole style,
hurricane at the back of your throat,
slurring vowels Paris slick and *soyeux,*
or smooth as water in a well, no impulse
to lean into your own reflection.

Hand over your self so that I might hand it back to you,
in the kitchen's darkness where touch is located in smell:
Finger to lips, Manzanilla olives; knee to knee is salt and cough
of pepper; hand to hip is amaryllis blooming in the window
like a fire show; odor of La Vita Dolcetto and snow,
its milk glass glazing trees, glinting in the margin

between stoplights and stars. To hell with mysticism
and ghosts and vapor, I want what I can grasp onto. Dig into.
Loam, a layer of clay beneath skin. Mud
stiffening our hair until we are statues of dirt; small
cuts on our bodies so that we may wash
and heal. So we might seal the foul and the fair together

when we ransack one another in a field of lobelia, milk vetch
while turkey vultures inch closer, sniffing us out,
smelling blood on us, and breath on us
so they fly back to the fringe of the field. And wait.
As we bite and bleed, taut in cobalt dark,
beneath a rain that falls like pollen and rusted chains.

Pretty White Dress

Hey ladybird lurking,
what's a fuzzy to you

and a fizzy to him?
Calligraphy or filigree

on the shield of a Viking.
He's aloof as a sawtooth.

He can't yodel or sing.
He's a killer Godzilla,

a teapot signaling steam.
A telltale heart, a deadly dart.

It's a Harlequin romance,
a dizzy and a doozy of a dance.

He's a dense lens, a frigate
on a frozen ocean.

You're a whirl of a girl, pearl
and vertigo, marbled star.

He's a conversation in the dark
ardor of a parked car,

smelling of mint and gin
in a seaside citadel

gliding down your pretty
white dress with a pen.

III.

THE SKY'S SONG

The Alpine flower was saying to the shell : "you gleam"
The shell said to the sea : "you ring"
The sea said to the boat : "you tremble"
The boat said to the fire : "you glitter"
The fire said to me : "I ring less than her name in your love"
The shell said to me : "I gleam less than the phosphorus of
    desire in your hollow dream"
The Alpine flower said to me : "She is beautiful"
I said : "She is beautiful, she is beautiful, she is moving."

—Robert Desnos

One Swallow Doesn't Make a Summer

1. A poem is
cuttlebone. Sugarcube.
It's a fiction. A glass of milk.
Baudelaire's concubine. An eager
sugar. A lunar reader.
A diary tax. Conflation of cupboard
and springboard. Conquistador and concerto.
A way of happening, a mouth. A landscape
drowsy, full of contradictions and peach trees.
A song, an urn, the ashcan
of imagine. Glass spittoon, a broken
arm. The elegance of the letter *f.*
Green noise of teeth, their
clackclack at night when the maids
are sleeping.

2. Poem marry me.
My absinthe bride-to-be
bury me in a barn with hair
husks, pollen dust.
Your eyes chasuble blue.
Sugar beet stench around your neck.
Widow cluster. Working
on the curtains, the wedding-ring quilts.
You quit us. And I was glad.
With your sad magnetic face around your aging lace.

3. Poetry's two-
lipped, sloe-black
and cobalt. Spasmodic.
Her bakelite bracelets
jangling. *Random patterning*
within a simple phenomenal system.
Sipping slivovitz on the terrace, she was
seized with *mal de mer* though she wasn't at sea.

4. Shush.
The windows are waking us
from revisionist dreams. Maize light
raising us from deep sea sleep.
Your words are seaspray,
agave. You are wafer weight
in my lightning mouth. I burn you
to strawberry. Leaf-lake. Glass bird
don't break.

The Insinuation of Lakes in
"The Garden of Mourners"

In bowers of trees, birdsong is a lament
Say smear, rain, tears
in the eye of a cockatoo

or a tourniquet, depending on the night's narrative.
Say wet, writhe, hydrangea, despair
of trees in February

A scene: you lying in a field, sea-green and bristling with corn,
Say sky, jeremiad, ferric
odor of storms and bogs

studying the distance between elbow and index finger
Say intercostal, coast, lush,
susurrus of wind-whipped grasses

beneath a cotillion of clouds in the garden of mourners:
Say glass, frost, hydrography,
a gauze of ice, lace

ghosts & flies & women that look like wolves lean over you
Say black, madness, South,
subterranean seascape of dreams

as you lie calm as a dollar bill in the palm of a priest.
Say Legba, bayou, voodoo, say crows
perch like curses on riverbanks

The air has the consistency of indium.
Say death,
say breathe

The moon wears a veil;
Say meet me on Lake Ponchartrain
in a cream convertible

while mirrors forget to reflect.
Say drown,
say drive

Residue

for Howe Gelb

Your voice is trafficking
toward me in the dark, sinuous
diamondback patterning itself
through sand. Steeped in heat
that sieves through my body
like Louisiana's rice fields and zydeco. Spangle
of rain on a pond; vengeance of insects.

(There is a man who lives two blocks down who barks at his car.)

It moves through my limbs like men
in uniform; a vinegarroon's sting; catching
the ear with the hundred eye-hooks
of a wedding gown. It lengthens
fingers and bristles like stalks of corn
in a field scattered with silvered
shells of armadillos.

(A man asking for change says, *Honey, why you look so sad?*
Smile, it ain't that bad.)

Spilling down my spine like coins
tossed in a coffee can. Sound of rain
seeping through a sheer nightgown, a woman
who lolls in the door of her back porch.
Soaked with whiskey and the sugarlick

whip of the blues. Your voice that tips
its hat back and says, *Darlin', I'll be damned.*

(When I was twelve, a priest tried to tongue my ear through the
confessional.)

Residue of sleet
on a trampoline, a silver screw undoing
what we thought we knew of tomorrow
which is nothing but jive-
dazzle and static. Melody of spells,
dove's blood and betony. It diffracts,
shattering like satinspar.

(In another room, a woman sings hymns along with the
television.)

Migrating over states, past tollbooths,
residing in fillings of men who drive pick-ups
away from the broken
bell of themselves. Men
who never stop moving. Voices, barbed
wire where sparrows impale feathered breasts
drawn to the clang of human longing.

(Get the fuck away from me! a couple argues in the hallway.)

Your voice that reaches me in sleep, sprouts
tubers and roots in my limbs, rests in the windows
of my hands. Alluvial lisp
licking insides of skin. An avalanche

of candelabras, stars
arcing through the dark. Your voice:
A forest. A cedilla. A film I should've been in.

The Siren's Dream

I dreamed of orangewood
as you exited my eyes
an apparition, a photoemission.

I'm still supine on the divan
as you take shape: heavy
precipitation, then an ocean

cove uninhabited for centuries.
Am I nothing
but a body floating

on the clear mist of citrus?
You fill the room with water and I
fall, elevator-style

into the green-glass sea,

shattering my knees. Glacé—
blood on bone, candied
orange. You suck the sun

into a cone, leave a green stain
as you funnel through
history while I stay

fastened to the observation
post of this listless century
offering sailors, their

scurvied ghosts, lemons
and lamentations pen-knifed
with viridian into skin-shadows

suspended like snow over the ocean.

Hydrophobia

Cornflowers fringe the river like lashes.
I am lonely, you concede. Leaves

adhere to your back in mottled tongues;
air articulates your face with odor of roasted

apples, evening's end. In second-story windows,
girls in fine coal dresses undress, scrim of their slips

lemon light: thin as a bone-button that unfastens
the sky. Blue door on a black house, your body

like glass: a pitcher of violets, twilight, a blue fruit
abandoned. An ice skate floats by on the river's ear.

Do you hear the current's assembly: a comb,
a greenfinch, plastic lids, an index finger, a fishing

lure, a mirror fragment containing the tumult of water
and bodies. Listen to the river's hiss; metal swallows

clip the air. Hunters in bright orange vests
approach you as though you were a ghost deer.

Terroir

The grape is the informant
with names recalling Estruscan
warriors: Piedmont's Barolo—terracotta
dense scented with truffles, smoke,
rose; Dolcetto, Barbaresco: earth first,

then smooth fruit. In France, dusty
lusciousness of Pouilly-Fuisse,
Viognier—pear, butterscotch, toasted
oak. Honey patina on wineglass.

Cabernet Sauvignon, purple
plush on tongue; currant stained
glass, teeth—swirl and first smell: absolute
imagery   nothing sexier than kissing a woman
sipping red wine

David declares
briar berries and crushed spices
the mouth a glass
skin and spillage

shoulders, Bordeaux; no shoulders, Burgundy

revered as blood once was thought
to arouse bravery if drunk
from skulls of conquered warriors

"wine is mutilating, surgical,
                          it transmutes and delivers"

a fat glass of cab served with steak au poivre
like an ambassador smoothing the stitch
between two continents

"it can serve as an alibi
                    to dream as well as reality"

the myth of it
is difficult to escape: Dionysus dips
his fingers into a chalice, smears claret across his face,
ferric smell: moss and boysenberry

David drinks it from the woman's mouth
instead of a glass; drops the size
of seeds accumulate on lips
like whispers: *here, taste this, be this*

Courting Procrustes

you are the rim of night in the denouement
of a day that started as a stutter of sun, then rain

wreckage, bed of wet petals, the unsaid,
insinuation of sleeping men

lover, let me listen in
to the blood meridian

outside, wet grass captured by moonlight
appears as endless fields of shattered glass and apples

now, the only sound the stridulation of spiders,
crush of bones in their purse of skin

the stretch of flesh is like linen pressed into hands
of lachrymose ladies at the opera

where the heroine waits for forty days
and forty nights for her lover to return

unaware as the audience is aware
that her young lad has lost his feet

and will not be returning with a bloom
of gardenias and a ring, containment

is the key to contentment,
measurement is your gift to the haphazard

impulse in each one of us,
all night I dream of dismemberments

but you remain next to me as I wipe tears
or sweat, I no longer know which,

from my darkness that will not halt,
I am drawn to your preparations

actions, Honey, any myth
can move his mouth

The Disease of Pronouns

I

She says sunscald, shutter
and scythe. Yellow

breath. He says emeralds
and venom. Almond

odor and bucolic
songs to Trakl.

She says I'm a threnody. You
are black bamboo.

Sapphire wire coiled
around a salamander's throat.

——

tiger   ice   orange

night   hyacinth

Glass and gold
vermouth. Purple

crepe myrtle. He says:

The ocean slanted orange.
The moon a room of white paint,
plaster saint, butcher's broom.
Thumbprints & lint stain the walls;
pressed against the window sill,
a ghost gum withers.

She says: this is getting old

He says: what are years

to the coelogyne's chainlike
racemes and sinister
glistening lips?

II

She says dogwood redwood driftwood orangewood

you are my rhetorical device   graveyard shift
electromagnetic wave   emetic
crepe suzette   spinal anesthetic

jade green moss green pea green sage green horror movie green

____

He says: you're my avant-garde get-well card

my photoelectric cell   superficial middle cerebral vein
champagne truffle   black morel
infrared   interbred   ultraviolet light

She says: what's the difference between flammable and
inflammable

——

you're my flash flood leaf bud, my trouser cuff, my Malacca
cane, my cloudless lovely weathervane

——

He says: your body's a flotation device

——

She says: fertility is a ribbon

Freeze Frame, with Forsythia

You will bind me
in an aquarelle, my skin
blue as Canterbury bells. Call me
mademoiselle before you execute, like the hand-
tinted photo of the dancer, Margarete Gertrud Zelle, arms
scissoring the air, fending bullets and flowers as she pirouettes.

You will find me
in the zero hour sipping
a whiskey sour with a cherry, my hair
yellow, not sallow or frizzed like Bishop's flower.
In a bell-shaped dress trimmed in snow-white florets, I smell
of fever, soil as I pose in the doorcase. You refer to me as daughter

of gnawed bones.
I am property of _____.
A profile in the slanted rain. I am
versatile. You call me Lily of the Nile, fingering
umbels as you scour the floor in search of my shadow. Hours
sift and flow and form a canted frame where you lean on one elbow

statuesque as a window
sash. You've captured me,
you say, mid-bloom, in your eye
frame, in the process of photograph and pose
and polyphonic prose, the kitchen lit by my ante-
bellum skirt, the yellow spikes of forsythia going up in flame.

Spectacle: Possession

1

A woman wears a blue dress. It is
Sunday. Red cardinals sing
along the sill. She cuts
her neck with an electric
carving knife. A woman is blue.
She is red. She wears
the Sunday blues. Carves
cardinals into an electric
red dress. Her neck
sings electric. Sunday wears on.
A knife sings before it cuts.
On the sill, Sunday carves
the necks of cardinals. Knives
wear red. Sunday dresses
along the sill. *Sing*
said the cardinal.
Sing said the knife.
A woman is electric.
Her neck is a sill.
Cardinals sing the Sunday
reds in her electric neck.
A woman is a carving.
A woman is a knife.
A woman.

2
A woman rises to a knock at her door,
a stone strikes her head as her ex-
husband plunges in, clutching
a rock and a carving
knife. He can't cope
with a prefix meaning *no longer*
or *lacking* so he whittles it
from her forehead, criss-
crossing her face with a blade
made for slicing steak.

Their thirteen-year-old daughter witnesses
from a corner, strapped to her
shadow in shock, her mouth
open, spilling the word *stop*
that circles the room in a boomerang
returning to splinter her throat, her father's
ears. The man looks up from his white
shirt, Rolex, ox-blood Gucci shoes
splashed with his ex-wife and says
I'm sorry to his daughter as the woman's
breath jags from collapsed lungs.

3
I am always burying something:
cardinals with shattered wings,
orange peels, smell of your dress
as it dries on the windowsill.

You come to me bearing
poppies, birds and glass,
a carving knife.
Your body a hieroglyph.

You want me to whittle you
down into an amulet;
a tooth necklace to
wear as a token.

In the kitchen's carnivorous light,
you and I are too much alike:
the skull's opalescent curve,
milkweed smelling skeleton,

bones tattered as lace.
Like lightning. Electric.
When I move you carve
yourself out of me

humming the mean reds
and the Sunday blues.
Sing say the birds.
Sing say the bones.

NOTES

"Robert Desnos and the Hummingbird"
J'ai tant rêvé de toi que tu perds ta réalité (I have dreamed of you so often that you lose your reality) is the first line of Robert Desnos' poem *J'ai tant rêvé de toi* in *Corps et biens.*

"There Are Wolves That Sit at the Feet of Men"
This title, discovered in French, *Il y a des loups qui s'assoient aux pieds de l'homme,* is taken from *Canto Nocturna Peregrini Aviumque* by Adam Makkai.

"The OED Defines Red-Hot"
Quoted lines are excerpted from the *Oxford English Dictionary, 2nd Edition* (except *coral nails, crimson lips*).

"Viewing Rain from a Hospital Bed"
This poem is a response to Denise Levertov's "The Wings." Thanks to her for providing the exoskeleton.

"Pretty White Dress"
Thanks to Tim Rutili for the title as well as the phrase "trout silk."

"*Terroir*"
Quoted material is from Roland Barthes' essay "Milk and Wine" in *Mythologies.* Italicized material is mine.

"One Swallow Doesn't Make a Summer"
A way of happening, a mouth is from "In Memory of W.B. Yeats" by W.H. Auden. *Random patterning within a simple*

phenomenal system comes from "The Chaos of Metafiction," from *Chaos and Order* by Peter Stoicheff.

"The Insinuation of Lakes in 'The Garden of Mourners'"
Thanks to Tony Fitzpatrick and his painting "The Garden of Mourners" that inspired the poem.

"Spectacle: Possession"
The title and some of the material in the first section make reference to Andrzej Zulawki's film *Possession*. This poem is dedicated to Mary Glenn.

——

The excerpt from "Under the Willows" and the poem "The Sky's Song" are from Robert Desnos' *Corps et biens*. Translations are mine.

THE AUTHOR

SIMONE MUENCH is poetry editor of *ACM*. Her poems have appeared in *Notre Dame Review, Poetry, Indiana Review, The Paris Review, The Bellingham Review,* and *POOL.* Her book *The Air Lost in Breathing* received the Marianne Moore Prize for Poetry from Helicon Nine in 2000. New Michigan Press released her chapbook *Notebook. Knife. Mentholatum.* in 2003. Currently, she is Assistant Professor at Lewis University as well as a doctoral student at the University of Illinois at Chicago. Recently, she was one of the Fine Lines winners co-sponsored by Olay and the Poetry Society of America; her winning poem will appear as part of the Poetry in Motion series. You can visit her Website at: www.simonemuench.com.